the
parenting
children
course

**for those parenting
0 to 10-year-olds**

> Leaders' Guide

ISBN: 978 1 905887 87 3

Published by Alpha International, HTB Brompton Road, London SW7 1JA.

Email: publications@alpha.org

relationshipcentral.org

Contents

Welcome

We're so glad that you've decided to run The Parenting Children Course and we hope you enjoy the experience as much as we do. Parents feel under more pressure than ever today and many are in need of help and support. Seeing them grow in confidence and feel less isolated through doing the course has made us want to keep going and to make this resource available to others to run in their home, community or church.

This Leaders' Guide is designed to help you to run a successful course. It is important that those who lead the discussions are familiar with the key ingredients of the course and the role of the small group hosts. It is also useful as a quick reference. We find it helpful to have it with us when we are running a session as the checklists and timetables help to keep us on track.

If you start to run a course, please register it online at **relationshipcentral.org**. This enables potential guests who live in your area to find a course nearby. It also enables us to let you know of ways in which we can support you.

Please do contact us if you have any questions and do let us know how you get on. We love to hear feedback from other courses.

Nicky and Sila Lee
Creators of The Parenting Children Course

Introduction

The Parenting Children Course, designed for those parenting children up to ten years old, was started at HTB, London, in 1990 and the material was first published in 2011. We have had many requests from people all around the world wanting to use this resource as well as The Parenting Teenagers Course, designed for those parenting eleven to eighteen-year-olds.

The course is for any parent or carer of children, whether they consider themselves to have strong parenting skills or are struggling, and whether they are expecting their first child, are a single parent or a step-parent. Guests can come alone or as a couple. The practical tools of the course are applicable to everyone who has responsibility for a child or children up to ten years old.

The course is made up of five weekly sessions lasting two-and-a-half hours, including the meal. However, the course can be run over ten sessions of one-and-a-half hours by splitting each session into two. With this is mind, each session talk has been divided into two parts on the DVD.

Each session ideally starts with something to eat and drink, as this gives guests a chance to relax and talk to other parents in a friendly, welcoming setting. Creating a great atmosphere is an important part of the course. Equally important is the reassurance for guests that nobody will have to disclose any information about their home life/parenting that they do not wish to. Many people, however, have discovered that discussing their experiences with fellow parents in a small group is one of the great benefits of the course.

After the meal, the leaders welcome the guests, give any notices and then provide an opportunity for a quick review of the previous session(s). They then show the relevant section of the DVD or give the talks themselves.

During each session there are breaks in the talks to give the guests an opportunity to discuss the issues that have been raised. For courses with more than ten guests, it is best to divide into two or more smaller groups. The groups are organised according to the age of the guests' oldest child. Each small group needs a host who acts as a facilitator for the discussion.

The course is designed so that it is easy to run, particularly when using the DVDs. You may decide to do your own talks eventually, but we would recommend starting with the DVDs as this means you can concentrate on hosting your guests and creating the right atmosphere.

Whichever way you decide to run the course, you will need to provide a guest manual for each person. These contain the questions for the group discussions and the exercises that the guests fill in during and after each session.

Using the DVDs

All the sessions of the course are available on DVD. Nicky and Sila's talks were filmed in a TV studio and each session includes street interviews and filmed clips of parenting experts as well as 'sofa' families, which comprise parents and children talking about their experiences of parenting and being parented.

The DVDs indicate when to pause for an exercise break or discussion. You can see the timings of these listed in the timetable for each session on pages 22–40 of this guide.

Giving live talks

If you are giving live talks, they should ideally be presented by a mother and a father. To prepare:
- watch the DVD of the particular session. You may also want to read the relevant section of *The Parenting Book*
- decide who will do each section of the talk, ensuring that you both have a turn to speak as it is helpful to have the perspective of a father and a mother on the different topics. You will

generally not be able to swap back and forth between you as frequently as on the DVDs

- agree on what stories you are going to share from your own family. Be sure these would not embarrass your children now or in the future. Tell stories against yourself, not against your children or the other parent
- it is possible to play in some of the filmed clips of parenting experts and the 'sofa' families by using the 'Filmed Clip Inserts' on the DVDs
- decide which clips to play in. There will not be time to use them all

Structure of a typical session

Five-week courses

The whole session, including the meal, lasts approximately two-and-a-half hours. We strongly suggest that you do not shorten the length of the discussions as these are often the most beneficial aspect of the course. Pages 22–31 show suggested timings for five-week courses.

Ten-week courses

Each of the five sessions is divided into two roughly equal parts, allowing the course to be run over ten weeks with each session lasting approximately one-and-a-half hours. Pages 32–40 show suggested timings for ten-week courses.

1. Welcome

Some guests are apprehensive when they first arrive, so a drink and a warm welcome will help them to feel relaxed.

> **Helpful tip:**
> *Men in particular can be hesitant about coming on the course so having other men to welcome them can make a big difference.*

2. The meal

Evening courses

The meal is an important time for guests to get to know other parents, to relax after work or putting children to bed, and to be put at their ease. It is crucial to create a warm, friendly atmosphere. It is generally best to serve a main course and then to serve cakes, biscuits or brownies with coffee and tea half way through the evening during the fifteen-minute exercise/discussion.

Morning courses

The meal could be breakfast or a snack and consist of tea and coffee, pastries, fruit and yoghurt, muesli, muffins, cakes and biscuits etc. As with courses run in the evening, the meal provides an opportunity for guests to relax and meet other parents/carers of children.

3. Notices and review

From Week 2 onwards guests are given a few minutes to review the previous session(s). *The Parenting Children Course Guest Manual* contains a summary of what has already been covered. The guests can share their thoughts and experiences in twos or threes, or as a small group.

4. Talk (Part 1) and short exercises/discussions

Five-week courses

The talk for each session is divided into two parts. Each part is approximately 30 minutes and the DVDs indicate clearly when to pause between the parts. Following Part 1 there is a fifteen-minute break when the guests are served tea or coffee and something to eat such as brownies, cakes or biscuits. Sometimes there is an exercise in the manual to complete and then to discuss, either as a small group or in twos or threes. (Discussing in twos or threes allows couples who are parenting together to discuss an issue with each other, while those parenting on their own can discuss with one or two others.)

Ten-week courses

Either Part 1 or Part 2 is played, depending on which week it is. When using Part 1, the short exercise/discussion is extended from fifteen minutes to at least half an hour, to allow for a group discussion. The manual has questions marked 'For ten-week courses only'.

5. Talk (Part 2)

Five-week courses

The session continues with Part 2 of the talk. If the guests are midway through discussing a topic that is important to one or more of them, the small group hosts can pick this up again in the longer discussion at the end of the evening. This works better than delaying Part 2 and having to shorten the last discussion. Sometimes the talk in Part 2 will help the discussion.

6. Group discussion

Five- and ten-week courses

These take place for half an hour or so at the end of each session. Small groups are led by small group hosts, who facilitate the discussion using the 'Small group discussion' questions in the guest manual as a guide. The aim is not to have all the answers, rather to give every guest the opportunity to speak. The hosts may occasionally share from their own experiences when appropriate. Arranging the small groups according to the age of the guests' oldest child ensures that each small group is at a similar stage of parenting and parents have similar issues to discuss. If the small group host is a parent, he or she should ideally have a child at least as old as the children of the guests in their group.

7. Ending

Five- and ten-week courses

It is important to bring the session to an end by the time stated so that the guests feel comfortable leaving promptly. This is best done by the host stating what the time is and standing up, however animated or inconclusive the discussion may be at that point. Some parents will need to leave promptly after evening courses because of childcare arrangements, while after morning courses some will need to collect children from school, preschool or childcare.

Those who are not in a hurry may want to continue discussing an issue informally. Many of the issues raised during the small group discussion will not have a neat solution. Raising the issue and hearing the experiences of other parents can help guests to know that they are not alone in the challenges they are facing and to gain a longer perspective.

8. Homework

There are homework exercises in the manual for guests to complete between the sessions. These are an important part of the course as they help guests to apply the topics raised in the session to their own situation. (When encouraging guests to complete the homework, assure them it is not the sort that is taken in and marked!)

9. Feedback

Five- and ten-week courses

A questionnaire is available for distribution during the final session. This serves as a review of the course for the guests and provides helpful feedback for the leaders. Guests are asked to fill most of it in during the meal and then complete it at the end of the session. (The appropriate questionnaire can be downloaded from our website: **relationshipcentral.org**)

Creating the right atmosphere

A warm and welcoming environment is very important to the success of the course. It is essential that guests feel relaxed and are able to talk freely about sensitive issues. The right atmosphere helps to make this possible.

1. Choose the best venue

The key is to find a location that allows you to create a welcoming atmosphere and serve a meal:

- if you are running a small course, a home is usually the best location
- larger courses can be held in a church hall, restaurant, café after hours, school, hotel etc

2. Think friendly, fun and relaxed

- if the course is not held in a home and the space is unappealing, find someone who enjoys the challenge of transforming it to look welcoming, friendly and relaxed. Even the most uninspiring room can be turned into a great venue, with a little creativity
- chairs arranged in a circle for the small groups, ideally around a low coffee-style table, give each guest a sense of belonging (this is particularly helpful if they have come on their own) and make it easier to facilitate the small group discussions. This arrangement also helps guests to chat and build friendships more easily, both over the meal and during the discussions. They can turn their chairs if necessary for the talks. (See page 41 for a suggested room set-up)
- low lighting and background music during the meal and at the end help to create a relaxed atmosphere

3. Provide food

- serving food before the course gives guests the opportunity to unwind and get to know others.
- on evening courses it also means people can come straight from work without having to worry about eating before the course. We recommend serving the main course at the start of each session. Coffee, tea and a simple dessert, cake or biscuits can then be served during the short exercise/discussion midway through the evening

4. Give great service

- some guests worry about coming on The Parenting Children Course. Having a friendly team who go out of their way to make the guests feel welcome helps to put them at their ease
- on the five-week courses the leaders help to serve the coffee and tea during the short break. This is a sign to the guests that you care about them and that their family life is important to you

Helpful Tip:
Cover the low coffee-style table with a table cloth, table napkins, a flower and a candle as this adds a special touch and helps create a great atmosphere, like a restaurant.

Hosting the small groups

Small group hosts play a vital role in the guests' experience of the course. For courses that have more than one small group, it will be important to get the hosts together prior to the course to ensure that they understand their role in welcoming and hosting the guests throughout each session as well as facilitating the discussions. Each small group host should have a copy of this Leaders' Guide.

Ideally there should be two or more hosts per group, including at least one man and one woman if the group is made up of fathers and mothers.

1. The role of the hosts

- the main role of the small group hosts is to welcome and host the guests in their group, to introduce them to each other, to serve them tea or coffee, to find out how their week has been, and to facilitate the small group discussion during the last part of each session
- on the first session, during the first discussion, the small group host should encourage people to contribute only what they feel comfortable sharing with others. Ask the guests to respect the other members by keeping any personal information that is disclosed in the group confidential
- the small group hosts are not instructors. Their job is to get the conversation flowing and encourage discussion, not to teach the guests about parenting (the talks aim to do that!). Small group hosts are welcome to suggest ideas from their own experiences of parenting/caring for children, but they need to ensure that it is in line with the course material. Their aim is to be encouraging and affirming, so the most helpful way of sharing their own stories and tips is to use 'I' or 'We' statements (such as, 'I/We have found this helpful...') rather than instructional statements ('You need to stop doing that and do this instead'). Using 'I' statements leaves the guests free to agree or disagree with what the host has suggested, rather than feeling that they are being judged

2. Preparation

- the small group hosts should familiarise themselves with the questions in the guest manual ahead of each session
- they will also find it helpful to read *The Parenting Book* in advance of the course so that they are familiar with the topics the course covers. There is more material in the book than the course is able to cover. The book also covers parenting teenagers, so it will give the host a longer perspective

3. Practical details

- arrange the chairs so that guests can see and hear each other
- ensure the host(s) can see everyone
- provide adequate lighting so that guests can read the manual and write ideas down if they wish

- check ventilation so that the room is neither stuffy nor too cold
- keep to time – aim to start and end the discussion on time
- if the group has more than ten guests and there are enough hosts, it may be better to split the group in half so that more people get a chance to contribute

4. Groups can be ruined by two types of leadership
- weak leadership – not properly prepared, allows one person to do all the talking
- dominant leadership – does all the talking instead of giving others the opportunity to say what is on their mind

5. Ask open questions
- 'open questions' require more than a 'yes' or 'no' answer and allow for a variety of responses, eg: 'What's the greatest challenge you're facing right now as a parent?' 'What's the main reason you attended the course?' 'What do you hope to get out of the course?'
- use the questions in the guest manual to get the discussion going, unless one of the guests has already raised an issue that is of interest to most of the group
- do not feel you have to get through all the 'Small group discussion' questions in the guest manual. Use as many as you need to keep the discussion moving, drawing in as many of the group as possible
- if running short of time and the discussion has been around only one or two of the questions for discussion, leave a few minutes at the end to ask, 'Did anyone want to discuss one of the other questions in the manual?' If so, tell the group you will come back to that question on the following session (either during the meal or as part of the small group discussion)
- have some follow-up questions of your own ready in case the discussion dries up
- two basic questions are: 'What do you think?' and 'What do you feel about what you have just heard?'
- rather than answering a question from a guest, direct it back to the group by asking: 'What does everyone else think?'
- avoid being patronising. Treat everyone with respect and interest even though you may disagree with their views

6. Be prepared for questions

- if an issue is raised that is beyond your experience or knowledge, don't be afraid to say so. If necessary, tell the guest(s) you will investigate sources of information about the issue before the next session
- see if the issue is covered by *The Parenting Book* or try another of the books listed in the back of the guest manual. (There is further recommended reading on our website: **relationshipcentral.org**)
- come back to the issue the following week either by talking to the individual guest over the meal or by raising it again in the small group discussion
- if the issue requires professional help, encourage the guest to talk to a doctor or a trained counsellor

Making referrals

Prior to the course, leaders should discover any other local sources of help for issues that are beyond their experience and beyond the scope of the course.

Guests may wish to discuss with a trained counsellor an issue that has been raised by the course or another issue they are facing. For some parents, coming on The Parenting Children Course will be the first step in seeking help for their situation.

If possible, have the contact details of a counsellor who deals with parenting issues, an educational psychologist or a parenting coach. You may be able to find a counsellor in the UK through the British Association for Counselling and Psychotherapy, the Association of Christian Counsellors or the UK Council for Psychotherapy. Their child's school may have an educational psychologist to whom they can be referred. Otherwise recommend guests consult their doctor, particularly if the issue relates to their own or their child's physical or emotional health.

Promoting the course

To help advertise your course:

- get your church leader on board. Help the leadership of your church to catch the vision of the course and to see the benefits that it can bring to members of your church and to other parents in your area
- ask to have the course advertised from the front during Sunday services. Promote the course dates in every way you can through the church website and newsletter, on notice boards and through displaying invitations prominently
- use the promotional film clip (on **relationshipcentral.org**) to excite parents and other carers of children. This three-minute clip gives people a taste of what is covered on the course and creates an interest to find out more
- think of places that might be interested in displaying posters and course invitations (available on **alphashop.org** and **alphaprintshop.org**):
  - local churches
  - schools
  - doctors' surgeries
  - the local library
  - charity shops
- try to get an article about the course in your local newspaper, or an interview with your local radio station
- ask to display course invitations and/or posters in other places where parents are likely to go, such as:
  - newsagents
  - fitness centres
  - other local shops
  - the local leisure centre/swimming pool
- don't forget that the main reason people come on the course is through a personal recommendation. Make sure that on the last session everybody on the current course is offered invitations to the next course to give away. Encourage them to tell at least one other parent. In this way your course will grow organically
- register your course on **relationshipcentral.org** so that people who are looking for a local course online find yours

Quick checklist

As well as the timetable in this Leaders' Guide you will need the following:

☐ *The Parenting Children Course DVD* set

☐ *The Parenting Children Course Guest Manuals* (one per person)

☐ Music (and a way to play it) – to be used during the meal and at the end of each session. A playlist on an MP3 player is the easiest option

☐ Food and drinks (cold and hot, including coffee and tea)
  Evening courses – main course and brownies, cakes or biscuits
  Morning courses – breakfast or a mid-morning snack
  eg: pastries, fruit and yoghurt, cakes and biscuits

☐ Tables and chairs, suitable lighting, tablecloths, table napkins, candles, flowers and vases

☐ Plates, glasses, cups and cutlery

☐ Attendance list and name labels. Wearing name labels helps people to get to know each other. For larger courses, having the small group hosts' names (or Group 1, 2, 3 etc) written underneath the guests' names helps them to find the right group

☐ Pens

☐ Spare guest manuals for guests who forget to bring theirs back, with a blank piece of paper slipped in for guests to write their own notes (without marking the manual)

You may want to have a copy of The Parenting Book *(by Nicky and Sila Lee) to give to guests who want to follow up on a particular session, or give a copy to each guest and include it as part of the cost of the course.*

☐ Table to display some of the recommended books (optional)

☐ Spare DVD(s) of the course for guests who may have missed a session. These can be loaned with a deposit so you can replace any that are not returned

☐ DVD player

☐ TV, or screen and projector

☐ Speakers' lectern and microphone (for larger courses only)

Helpful Tip:
To make sure you have the best and most recently updated resources, we suggest you regularly check our website: **relationshipcentral.org**

Overview and timetable for five-week courses

(two-and-a-half-hour sessions)

Session 1 – Building Strong Foundations

1. Overview

Part 1 looks at what a family is for. It covers how the family should be a place of support for children, a place where there's plenty of fun, a place that gives children a moral compass and a place where they learn how to relate. The idea of a weekly 'Family Time', to have fun together regularly, is introduced. In Part 2, parents are encouraged to think about setting goals and having a vision for their family. The session then addresses how to establish a healthy family life through encouraging active play, enabling parental bonding through spending time with each child, and establishing healthy routines around mealtimes and bedtime.

2. Checklist

- materials from Quick checklist on pages 20–21

3. Timetable

(The timetable that follows is for courses being run in the evening. The starting time may, of course, be adjusted)

6.30   Leaders meet to pray together

6.45   Be ready! (Guests often arrive early for the first session.) Offer guests a drink

7.00   Meal (in their small groups, if there are more than ten guests on the course)

7.30   Welcome and notices

– *'Welcome to The Parenting Children Course. Each session will be a combination of talks and discussing parenting issues with other parents. But, relax! Be assured you will not be required to disclose anything private about your children or family life'*

- 'Let us know if you can't come for one of the sessions and we will loan you the DVD' (if available)
- 'If you have a concern about your parenting that is not covered by the course, we have the details of a local family counsellor we could put you in touch with'
- 'We'll spend the next few minutes going round the group and asking you to introduce yourself and the names and ages of your child or children. Then please say the main challenge you are facing as a parent/carer of children. As people will be sharing personal information about their family life, we ask that you would respect what others say by keeping it confidential to the group'

Note: The timings follow the exact length of the talks on the DVDs.

7.40   Start the DVD (or your live talk) – *Part 1: The role of the family* (33 minutes)

8.13   Exercise and discussion

'Please complete the exercise in your manual, Taking Stock of Your Parenting, *and then discuss what you have put in groups of two or three. If you are here as a couple, we suggest you discuss with your partner what you have put and talk about any changes you would like to make'*

(Small group hosts serve tea, coffee and dessert)

8.28   Talk – *Part 2: Patterns for a healthy family life* (32 minutes)

9.00   Discussion in small groups (see questions in the guest manual)

9.30   End punctually. Encourage guests to complete the Homework Exercises 1 and 2 in the guest manual before the next session. Remind them to bring their manuals back for the next session

Live talks: Finish session with a short prayer if appropriate. For example:
'Lord, we thank you so much for the gift of children. We thank you that family life is the best environment for children to grow up in. We pray that you would help each of us to make our families a place of support, a place of fun, a place where our children learn important values for life, and a place where they learn what loving others is all about. We ask this in Jesus' name, Amen'

Session 2 – Meeting our Children's Needs

1. Overview

In this session parents think about how to meet their children's needs. Part 1 introduces the idea of children having an 'emotional tank', which is kept full through knowing their parents' unconditional love. Gary Chapman's concept of the five love languages is used to show the different ways in which love can be expressed. The first two expressions of love, words and touch, are looked at in more detail. Part 2 covers the other three love languages: time, presents and actions. Parents are encouraged to work out which expression of love makes the most difference to their child(ren) as well as which of the love languages they find most difficult to give.

2. Checklist

- materials from Quick checklist on pages 20–21

3. Timetable

6.30 Leaders meet to pray together

6.45 Offer a drink to guests who arrive early

7.00 Meal in groups

7.30 Notices and review

- *'Welcome back if you were here for the first session. A special welcome if you're here for the first time'*

- *'There are spare manuals for you to borrow if you forgot to bring yours. Please write any notes on the blank sheet and then you can transfer these into your own manual later on'*

- *'We will start each session with a review of the previous session or sessions. Please look in your manual at the summary of what we covered last week. Talk in your group about what was most relevant for you and if you have organised any "Family Time" over this past week. If you did, how did it go?'*

7.45 Start the DVD (or your live talk) – *Part 1: Words and touch* (28 minutes)

8.13 Short discussion

'Discuss the questions in your manual in groups of two or three'

(Small group hosts serve tea, coffee and dessert)

8.28 Talk – *Part 2: Time, presents and actions* (27 minutes)

8.55 Discussion in small groups (see questions in the guest manual)

9.30 End punctually. Encourage guests to complete the Homework Exercises 1–4 in their manual before the next session

Live talks: Finish session with a short prayer if appropriate. For example:
'Lord, we thank you that you assure us of your love for us. We pray that you would show us how to love each of our children in such a way that they feel secure in our love, and are confident to build strong friendships and to look to the needs of others. We ask this in Jesus' name, Amen'

Session 3 – Setting Boundaries

1. Overview

This session looks at how parents can establish healthy boundaries. Part 1 compares different parenting styles (neglectful, authoritarian, indulgent and authoritative) and shows how a combination of warmth and firmness (authoritative parenting) is the most beneficial style for a child's healthy development. The concept of right and wrong choices is explained. Parents are encouraged to help their child(ren) take responsibility for their own actions from a young age. Part 2 addresses a number of practical ways that parents can stay in control of themselves while helping their child(ren) to make good choices. The session covers the importance of following through with appropriate consequences when a boundary is crossed. Parents are encouraged to work together whenever possible in setting boundaries.

2. Checklist

- materials from Quick checklist on pages 20–21

3. Timetable

- 6.30 Leaders meet to pray together
- 6.45 Offer a drink to guests who arrive early
- 7.00 Meal in groups
- 7.30 Notices and review
    - *'In the last session we looked at how we make our children feel loved. We recommend* The Five Love Languages of Children *by Gary Chapman and Ros Campbell for a greater understanding of showing love effectively to each child'*
    - *'Please look in your manual at the summary of what we covered last week. Discuss in your group if you have tried using one of the five love languages in a new way since then. If so, what was the effect?'*
- 7.45 Start the DVD (or your live talk) – *Part 1: Combining love and limits* (31 minutes)
- 8.16 Exercise and discussion

'Please complete the exercise in your manual, Natural Childishness, *and then discuss what you've put, in groups of two or three'*

(Small group leaders serve tea, coffee and dessert)

8.31 Talk – *Part 2: Helping our children make good choices*
(23 minutes)

8.54 Discussion in small groups (see questions in the guest manual)

9.30 End punctually. Encourage guests to complete the Homework Exercises 1 and 2 in the guest manual before the next session

Live talks: Finish session with a short prayer if appropriate. For example:
'Lord, we thank you that you show us the best ways to live. We ask that you would help us to see clearly how to put right boundaries in place for our children. We pray that you would help each parent with the particular challenges they're facing, and help them with this combination of showing warmth and firmness. We ask this in Jesus' name. Amen'

Session 4 – Teaching Healthy Relationships

1. Overview

This session addresses how we can teach our children to build healthy relationships. Children learn most about how to relate from their own family. What parents model has the greatest impact on children. Part 1 looks at how listening effectively is one of the most powerful skills to learn as a parent. 'Reflective listening' is practised in the exercise. Part 2 addresses how to handle our anger appropriately and how to help our children to handle theirs. The session finishes on the importance of modelling how to resolve conflict well, including making up through saying sorry and expressing forgiveness.

2. Checklist

- materials from Quick checklist on pages 20–21

3. Timetable

6.30   Leaders meet to pray together

6.45   Offer a drink to guests who arrive early

7.00   Meal in groups

7.30   Notices and review

   – *'Next week we will have some of the recommended books on sale. You can pay by cash/cheque/card'* (as applicable)

   – *'Please look in your manual at the summary of what we covered last week. Then try to think of an example of a boundary you needed to impose since then, and discuss in your group what the result was'*

7.45   Start the DVD (or your live talk) – *Part 1: Modelling and practising* (30 minutes)

8.15   Exercise and discussion.

   'Please complete the exercise in your manual, Reflective Listening, *in pairs. One of you pretends to be a child (aged between five and ten) and the other pretends to be the child's parent. The "child" says one of the remarks listed in the manual, such as "Everyone else in my class is better at*

drawing than me." The "parent" reflects back what you think the child might be feeling by saying something like, "It sounds like you find drawing difficult." (As the parent, avoid giving advice or reassurance – that might be appropriate later in the conversation, but not yet.)

The child then indicates whether or not the parent has understood, so may say, "Yes, I can never do what the teacher tells us to do." The parent reflects back again with something like, "That must be annoying for you."

Continue the conversation for a minute or two. Then swap roles. Use another of the remarks and follow the instructions in your manual

When you've finished, discuss in twos or threes what it felt like to be listened to as the "child" and how easy or difficult you found it as the "parent" to reflect back the child's feelings. Then look at question 2 in your manuals about whether you've developed any unhelpful listening habits, such as listening to one child more attentively than to another'

(Small group hosts serve tea, coffee and dessert)

8.30 Talk – *Part 2: Handling anger (our and theirs)* (27 minutes)

8.57 Discussion in small groups (see questions in the guest manual)

9.30 End punctually. Encourage guests to complete Homework Exercises 1 and 2 in their manual before the next session

Live talks: Finish session with a short prayer if appropriate. For example:
'Lord, we thank you for your patience and kindness towards us. Thank you that you forgive us when we get it wrong. We pray that in our homes apologies and forgiveness would be commonplace. Help us to resolve conflict well and to give our children a model of handling anger in a healthy way. We ask this in Jesus' name, Amen'

Session 5 – Our Long-Term Aim

1. Overview

The final session explores our long-term goals for our family, and how parents are aiming to train their children for healthy independence. Part 1 helps parents to recognise symptoms of unhealthy control in themselves. There is practical advice on helping children make good choices in areas such as drugs, alcohol, the Internet and sex. Part 2 addresses how to pass on our beliefs and values to our children and looks at the benefits of having family traditions, routines and rituals for creating a sense of secure identity and through which positive values are transmitted to children.

2. Checklist

- materials from Quick checklist on pages 20–21

3. Timetable

6.30   Leaders meet to pray together

6.45   Offer a drink to guests who arrive early

7.00   Meal in groups

7.30   Notices (as applicable) and review

- *'Do please take advantage of the opportunity to buy some of the recommended books at the end of the session'*

- *'Please take as many invitations for the next Parenting Children Course as you like to give to anyone who you think would be interested in coming'*

- *'The Marriage Course is a very good follow-up to this course for those who are parenting as a couple. If this applies to you, please come on our next course and take more invitations to give to others'*

- *'The Alpha course provides an opportunity to explore the meaning of life and to discuss the claims of the Christian faith. Doing Alpha has helped many parents to work out what beliefs and values they want to pass on to their children. Please take an invitation to our next course'*

– *'It would be helpful if you could take a few minutes to complete the feedback questionnaire. This acts as a review for you of the whole course and your comments will help us to run the course more effectively in the future. We will give you a few minutes to fill in your comments on this session before we finish'*

A copy of the questionnaire can be downloaded from our website: **relationshipcentral.org**

7.45 Start the DVD (or your live talk) – *Part 1: Encouraging responsibility* (30 minutes)

8.15 Exercise 1 and discussion

'Please complete the exercise Letting Go Gradually *and then discuss in groups of two or three'*

(Small group hosts serve tea, coffee and dessert)

8.30 Talk – *Part 2: Passing on beliefs and values* (30 minutes)

9.00 Discussion in small groups (see questions in the guest manual)

9.30 End punctually. Encourage guests to complete the Homework Exercises 1–3 in the guest manual

Live talks: Finish session with a short prayer if appropriate. For example:

'Lord, we thank you that you know and love every child represented by those doing this course. Thank you that we can call out to you for them. Thank you that you hear our prayers. Thank you for all the other people, besides us as parents, who help to guide and shape our children. We pray that you would fulfil your purposes for each child. Please help us to trust you with our children and to put our hopes and longings into your hands. May we create homes that are loving and secure, in which our children are free to become the unique people you have created them to be. We ask this in Jesus' name. Amen'

Ask the guests to complete the questionnaire and hand it in before they leave.

Overview and timetable for
ten-week courses

(one-and-a-half-hour sessions)

Some course leaders prefer to run the course over ten weeks rather than five. This might be the case if you are running it in the morning for parents who have children to pick up before midday, or if your timings are restricted for some other reason. The five sessions are split into Part 1 and Part 2 and one part only is used each week.

(The timetable that follows is for courses being run in the morning.)

Note: The timings follow the exact length of the talks on the DVDs

Week 1
Session 1 – Building Strong Foundations, Part 1

10.00   Welcome guests and offer something to eat and drink
(coffee, tea, pastries, fruit and yoghurt, muesli, muffins etc)

10.15   Welcome and notices

– *'Welcome to The Parenting Children Course. Each session will be a combination of talks and discussing parenting issues with other parents. But, relax! Be assured you will not be required to disclose anything private about your children or family life'*

– *'Let us know if you can't come for one of the mornings and we will loan you the DVD' (if available)*

– *'If you have a concern about your parenting that is not covered by the course, we have the details of a local family counsellor we could put you in touch with'*

– *'We'll spend the next few minutes going round the group(s) asking you to introduce yourself and the names and ages of your child or children. Then please say the main challenge you are facing as a parent/carer of children'*

10.25   Start the DVD (or your live talk) – *Session 1 Part 1: The role of the family* (33 minutes)

10.58   Ask guests to complete the exercise *Taking Stock of Our Parenting* and then have a small group discussion (see questions for ten-week courses in the guest manual)

11.30   End punctually. Encourage guests to complete Exercise 1 of the homework before next time.

         If appropriate, finish with a short prayer.
         (There is no prayer at the end of Part 1 on the DVD.)
         For example:
         'Lord, we thank you for every child represented on this course by a parent or carer. We pray that our children's experience of family life would provide them with a deep sense of security, self-worth and significance. Please help us to make our home a place where our children learn to build strong relationships. We ask this in Jesus' name, Amen'

Week 2
Session 1 – Building Strong Foundations, Part 2

10.00   Welcome guests and offer something to eat and drink

10.15   Notices and review

         – *'Welcome back if you were here for the first session. A special welcome if you are here for the first time'*

         – *'There are spare manuals for you to borrow if you forgot to bring yours. Please write any notes on the blank sheet and then you can transfer these into your own manual later on'*

         – *'We will start each session with a quick review of the previous session or sessions. Please look back in your manual to remind yourself what we covered on Week 1. Then discuss (as a group, or with one or two others) whether you have made any changes in your parenting since last week'*

10.25 Start the DVD (or your live talk) – *Session 1 Part 2: Patterns for a healthy family life* (32 minutes)

10.57 Small group discussion (see questions for ten-week courses in the guest manual)

11.30 End punctually. Encourage the guests to complete Exercise 2 of the homework before next time

Live talks: If appropriate, finish the session with a short prayer. For example:
'Lord, we thank you that you assure us of your love for us. We pray that you would show us how to love each of our children in such a way that they feel secure in our love, and are confident to build strong friendships and to look to the needs of others. We ask this in Jesus' name, Amen'

Week 3
Session 2 – Meeting our Children's Needs, Part 1

10.00 Welcome guests and offer something to eat and drink

10.15 Review
'Look in your manual at a summary of what has been covered so far. Tell somebody else in your group what has been most relevant for you and if you organised any "Family Time" over this past week. If so, talk about how it went'

10.25 Start the DVD (or your live talk) – *Session 2 Part 1: The five love languages – words and touch* (28 minutes)

10.53 Small group discussion (see questions for ten-week courses in the guest manual)

11.30 End punctually. Encourage the guests to complete Exercises 1 and 2 of the homework before next time

If appropriate, finish the session with a short prayer. For example:
'Lord, we thank you that each of us has been created to receive and to give love. We pray that you would help us to show love to our children with our words and through our touch in the way that will make them feel loved. We ask this in Jesus' name, Amen'

Week 4
Session 2 – Meeting our Children's Needs, Part 2

10.00 Welcome guests and offer something to eat and drink

10.15 Review

'Discuss with one or two others whether showing love through affirming words and affectionate touch has made a difference to your child or children'

10.25 Start the DVD (or your live talk) – *Session 2 Part 2: The five love languages – time, presents and actions* (27 minutes)

10.52 Small group discussion (see questions for ten-week courses in the guest manual)

11.30 End punctually. Encourage the guests to complete Exercises 3 and 4 of the homework before next time

Live talks: If appropriate, finish the session with a short prayer. For example:
'Lord, we thank you that you assure us of your love for us. We pray that you would show us how to love each of our children in such a way that they feel secure in our love, and are confident to build strong friendships and to look to the needs of others. We ask this in Jesus' name, Amen'

Week 5
Session 3 – Setting Boundaries, Part 1

10.00 Welcome guests and offer something to eat and drink

10.15 Review

'Discuss whether you have tried using any of the five love languages this week. If so, talk about the effect on your child or children'

10.25 Start the DVD (or your live talk) – *Session 3 Part 1: Combining love and limits* (31 minutes)

10.56 Exercise and discussion
Ask guests to complete the exercise *Natural Childishness* and then have a small group discussion (see questions for ten-week courses in the guest manual)

11.30 End punctually. Encourage guests to complete Exercise 1 of the homework before next time

Live talks: If appropriate, finish the session with a short prayer. For example:

'Lord, we thank you that you show us right from wrong. We pray that you would help us to teach our children a sense of responsibility for their actions. Please help us to combine warmth and firmness and give us self-control as we set boundaries for our children. We ask this in Jesus' name, Amen'

Week 6
Session 3 – Setting Boundaries, Part 2

10.00 Welcome guests and offer something to eat and drink

10.15 Review

'Discuss with one or two others what was most helpful for you from the session last week'

10.25 Start the DVD (or your live talk) – *Session 3 Part 2: Helping our children make good choices* (23 minutes)

10.48 Small group discussion (see questions for ten-week courses in the guest manual)

11.30 End punctually. Encourage guests to complete Exercise 2 of the homework before next time

Live talks: If appropriate, finish the session with a short prayer. For example:

'Lord, we thank you that you show us the best ways to live. We ask that you would help us to see clearly how to put right boundaries in place for our children. We pray that you would help each parent with the particular challenges they're facing, and help them with this combination of showing warmth and firmness. We ask this in Jesus' name, Amen'

Week 7
Session 4 – Teaching Healthy Relationships, Part 1

10.00 Welcome guests with something to eat and drink

10.15 Review

'Think of an example of a boundary you needed to impose with a child this week. Discuss what the result was.'

10.25 Start the DVD (or your live talk) – *Session 4 Part 1: Modelling and practising relationships* (30 minutes)

10.55 Exercise and discussion

'Please complete the exercise in your manual, Reflective Listening, *in pairs. One of you pretends to be a child (aged between five and ten) and the other pretends to be the child's parent. The "child" says one of the remarks listed in the manual, such as "Everyone else in my class is better at drawing than me." The "parent" reflects back what you think the child might be feeling by saying something like, "It sounds like you find drawing difficult." (As the parent, avoid giving advice or reassurance – that may be appropriate later in the conversation, but not yet.)*

The child then indicates whether or not the parent has understood, so might say, "Yes, I can never do what the teacher tells us to do." The parent reflects back again with something like, "That must be annoying for you."

Continue the conversation for a minute or two. Then swap roles. Use another of the remarks and follow the instructions'

Then have a small group discussion (see questions for ten-week courses in the guest manual)

11.30 End punctually. Encourage guests to complete Exercise 1 of the homework before next time

Live talks: If appropriate, finish the session with a short prayer. For example:
'Lord, thank you that you listen to us when we call out to you. Please help us to be good at listening to our children, and may we grow in recognising and acknowledging what they are feeling. We ask this in Jesus' name, Amen'

Week 8
Session 4 – Teaching Healthy Relationships, Part 2

10.00   Welcome guests with something to eat and drink

10.15   Review

'Discuss whether you have become any better at listening to your child(ren). Did you try "reflecting back" what a child said this week? If so, what difference did it make?'

10.25   Start the DVD (or your live talk) – *Session 4 Part 2: Handling anger (ours and theirs)* (27 minutes)

10.52   Small group discussion (see questions for ten-week courses in the guest manual)

11.30   End punctually. Encourage guests to complete Exercise 2 of the homework before next time

Live talks: If appropriate, finish the session with a short prayer. For example:
'Lord, we thank you for your patience and kindness towards us. Thank you that you forgive us when we get it wrong. We pray that in our homes apologies and forgiveness would be commonplace. Help us to resolve conflict well and to give our children a model of handling anger in a healthy way. We ask this in Jesus' name, Amen'

Week 9
Session 5 – Our Long-Term Aim, Part 1

10.00   Welcome guests with something to eat and drink

10.15   Review

'Discuss what you realised about handling your own and your children's anger last week. What difference has it made?'

10.25   Start the DVD (or your live talk) – *Session 5 Part 1: Encouraging responsibility* (30 minutes)

10.55   Exercise and discussion

Ask guests to complete the exercise *Letting Go Gradually* and then have a small group discussion (see questions for ten-week courses in the guest manual)

11.30 End punctually. Encourage guests to complete Exercises 1 and 2 of the homework before next time

Live talks: If appropriate, finish the session with a short prayer. For example:
'Lord, we thank you that you guard and protect us. We pray that you would use us to guide and protect our children while helping them to take responsibility and to make good choices for their own actions. We ask this in Jesus' name, Amen'

Week 10
Session 5 – Our Long-Term Aim, Part 2

10.00 Welcome guests with something to eat and drink

10.15 Notices (as applicable) and review

– *'Do please take advantage of the opportunity to buy some of the recommended books at the end of the session'*

– *'Please take as many invitations for the next Parenting Children Course as you like to give to anyone you think would be interested in coming'*

– *'The Marriage Course is a very good follow up to this course for those who are parenting as a couple. If that applies to you, please come on our next course and take invitations to give to others'*

– *'The Alpha course provides an opportunity to explore the meaning of life and to discuss the claims of the Christian faith. Doing Alpha has helped many parents to work out what beliefs and values they want to pass on to their children. Please take an invitation to our next course'*

– *'It would be helpful if you could take a few minutes to complete the feedback questionnaire. This acts as a review for you of the whole course and your comments will help us to run the course more effectively in the future. We will give you a few minutes to fill in your comments on this session before we finish'*

A copy of the questionnaire can be downloaded from our website: **relationshipcentral.org**

10.30 Start the DVD (or your live talk) –
Session 5 Part 2: Passing on beliefs and values
(30 minutes)

11.00 Small group discussion (see questions for ten-week courses in the guest manual)

11.30 End punctually. Encourage guests to complete Exercise 3 of the homework

Ask guests to complete the feedback questionnaire and hand it in before they leave

Live talks: If appropriate, finish the session with a short prayer. For example:
'Lord, we thank you that you know and love every child represented by those doing this course. Thank you that we can call out to you for them. Thank you that you hear our prayers. Thank you for all the other people, besides us as parents, who help to guide and shape our children. We pray that you would fulfil your purposes for each child. Please help us to trust you with our children and to put our hopes and longings into your hands. May we create homes that are loving and secure, in which our children are free to become the unique people you have created them to be. We ask this in Jesus' name, Amen'

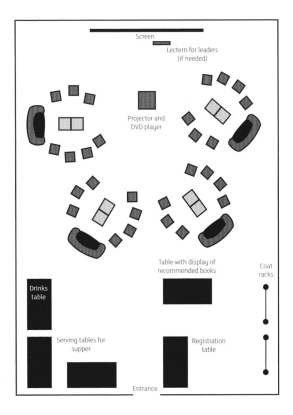

Note: the tables used for the small groups can be two small tables joined together (as indicated here) or one larger one.

Contact information

For information on The Marriage Course (for married or cohabitating couples), The Marriage Preparation Course (for engaged couples) or The Parenting Teenagers Course (for those parenting 11 to 18-year-olds), or for further information on The Parenting Children Course, please visit our website: **relationshipcentral.org**

For information about the Alpha course (for anyone wanting to enquire about the Christian faith), please see: **alpha.org**

Please feel free to contact us if we can be of assistance:
info@relationshipcentral.org
0845 644 7533

Other resources from Alpha International are available at your local Christian bookshop, from **alphashop.org** and **alphaprintshop.org**, or by phoning the Alpha Publications Hotline on **0845 758 1278**

Also by Nicky and Sila Lee

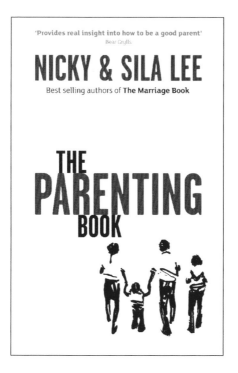

'Provides real insight into how to be a good parent'
Bear Grylls

NICKY & SILA LEE

Best selling authors of **The Marriage Book**

THE
PARENTING
BOOK

To order go to **alphashop.org**

ISBN 978 1 905887 36 1
Price £7.99

relationshipcentral.org